PREFACE

To the readers, Hi, hello. Thank you for purchasing my book 'Bipolar Fighter'.

I am very excited because my writing for the book 'Bipolar Fighter' has been completely finished and well produced for all readers, even though it took almost one year to finish it.

It is not because of difficult to write, but rather due to a lack of focus and disruptive mood swings that hindered the writing process.

I have observed that it is uncommon for individuals with mental illness to share their experiences with the public. Mental illness is often associated with stigma and shame.

Personally, I also feel a bit apprehensive about writing about this experience, concerned about touching on others' and my own sensibilities.

Nevertheless, I strive to uplift my spirit and share a bit of this experience with all of you who are willing to read my life story.

The World Health Organization (WHO) reports that half of all mental illnesses begin by the age of 14 and most of them are not diagnosed and untreated at an early stage. In terms of the burden of disease among adolescents or teenagers, depression problems are reported to be the third highest cause leading to mental health issues.

Surrounded by lush green paddy fields, the breathtaking natural panorama of Sekinchan, Selangor, Malaysia, is ideal for self-healing.

Individuals like myself always need to be in an alpha state, which is a state of calm mood. That's why whenever there's an opportunity, I seek out places for self-recovery.

It is not because I am constantly stressed, but rather to maintain tranquility so that I can function normally like any other person.

Maintaining my focus was the biggest challenge in completing this e-book. I drafted it in a workbook and wrote it in various places such as at home, in my car, and in the hospital ward.

It took me over a year to complete my life story, which spans 38 years. Mood swings were frequent, with depressive episodes followed by manic ones.

Since it is a life story, let's keep it relaxed and easygoing.

HAPPY READING!

TIMELINE: 1992-1998

CHILDHOOD

1) KINDERGARTEN

My story begins at the kindergarten level. It is highly significant to start from here to understand my entire journey. I attended Kindergarten in the town of Kota Jembal, Kota Bharu, Kelantan, Malaysia.

It was my first time holding a scroll, and perhaps also my last. Since then, I haven't had any experiences holding a scroll because I never graduated despite studying in many places.

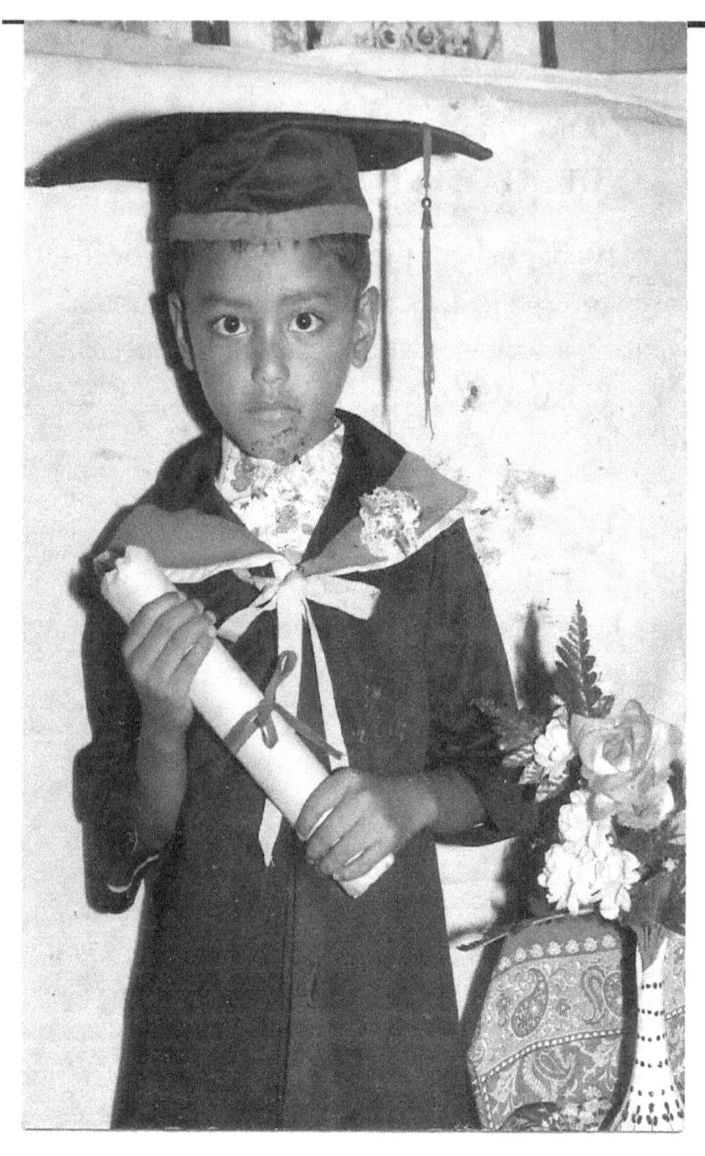

This picture was taken while playing the game of "tolak tin milo" (pushing the Milo tin).

Without this picture, I would not have a complete memory of playing this game. The game is from the 80s and 90s. It was quite nostalgic! It brings me back to the memories of carefree and joyful childhood days.

Childhood is indeed beautiful. There is no time to think about responsibilities or exerting energy to earn a living.

The only things to do were play and eat when feeling hungry. I sleep when I feel sleepy. Have a brief fight, then become friends again without holding grudges. Envy and jealousy are far away.

I remember my childhood with a deep sense of nostalgia.

One event that made me very happy was when my family and I went for picnics at the beach every weekend.

I remember how much fun it was to play on the beach, build sandcastles, swim in the sea, and enjoy quality time with my family.

Despite that, some moments made me feel sad and cry. One of those moments was when I lost my beloved pet, which is a cat that had been my faithful companion for years.

The sense of loss was profound and left a strong impression in my memory.

Although these events may have long passed, they remain stored in the deepest recesses of my memory.

They evoke a range of emotions, from joy to sadness, and I believe they are powerful enough to be recalled anytime, bringing either a smile or tears to my face.

Childhood memories are often cherished and evoke a mix of emotions. They hold the innocence, wonder, and experiences that form who we become.

From the simple joy of playing with friends to the warmth of family gatherings, these memories form the foundation of our identities.

In childhood, every moment feels like an adventure waiting to unfold. From climbing trees to chasing butterflies, each experience is filled with curiosity and excitement.

Even the smallest of things, like the sound of rain tapping on the window or the taste of ice cream on a hot summer day, hold a special place in our hearts.

Yet, childhood is not without its challenges. From scraped knees to the occasional disappointment, every hurdle teaches us resilience and strength.

It is in these moments of adversity that we learn valuable life lessons that stay with us into adulthood.

As we grow older, childhood memories become a source of comfort and nostalgia. They remind us of simpler times and the pure joy of living in the moment.

Whether it is flipping through old photo albums or sharing stories with loved ones, revisiting these memories brings a sense of warmth and connection.

In the end, childhood memories are more than just moments from the past – they are a part of who we are. They build our perspectives, influence our choices, and remind us of the beauty in life's simplest pleasures.

Try to recall the nostalgia of your childhood. If not laughter, surely there must be tears, remembering many soul-stirring events.

What events made you happy? Recall and feel it. And what moments made you sad and cry? These events are not lost in memory but deeply stored in the depths of memory and need to be recalled.

I am sure we will remember them and it is sweet enough for us to laugh or cry about now.

What I have remembered, I once had a growth on my neck. It grew and then burst, leaving a large and critical hole.

My mother said my condition at that time was life-threatening because it involved the respiratory tract. God extended my life till this day and allowed me to share this story with all of you.

Writing. This is my therapy, in facing the uncertainties of the mind that constantly battles with itself.

Since I am already writing, might as well continue and turn it into a book.

2) PRIMARY SCHOOL

I began my primary school in 1993. I was quite mischievous until I got punished by the prefect to the point of tears.

After that, I behaved well and became the favorite student of Cikgu Russinah binti Zamzam, my First Grade's teacher. I remember her name because she once offered me to marry her daughter.

By the time I reached Second Grade, things were a bit better. I started to excel in studies.

In Third Grade, I began to consistently rank in the top three of my class. During that time, I used to compete with a quiet girl named Liyana. If she got first place, I got second, and vice versa.

Sometimes, there would be other competitors who would 'steal' our rankings, but it was rare.

In Fourth Grade, I was selected as a school prefect, along with four boys and four girls. That was the usual practice in Fourth Grade.

When I think about it, I did not encounter any symptoms of Bipolar disorder during my time in primary school.

I could focus on studying and even rank in the top three of my class.

In Fifth Grade, everything went smoothly. Then came to the final year, Sixth Grade.

Year 1998. The year where I took my primary school's final examination (UPSR) before going to Secondary School.

Extra classes began. Homework piled up. I studied day and night. My life revolved around studying. I cycled to school every morning.

I did not go to the canteen during break time. I rarely visited the canteen in a year. I did not like crowded places, and till now I am still avoiding those places, including wedding ceremonies.

After the morning study session, there was a break. There wasn't enough time to go home. Then, there were additional classes in the afternoon.

Even before the exhaustion from studying disappeared, I had to return to school for evening classes.

When did I do my homework? I would wake up very early in the morning to finish my homework.

I automatically woke up around 4 or 5 in the morning because I knew my homework was not finished yet.

If it was not done, I could see the stern faces of the teachers one by one. If not, I would get caned, stand on the chair, or my sideburns get pulled.

The most embarrassing punishment was standing outside the classroom where everyone passing by could see. I had rather be caned than stand outside.

But there was something even scarier!

Standing under the scorching heat at the assembly area. Your brain could melt. This punishment was unforgettable.

Okay, homework done, then I had showered and get ready for school. I had taken my daily allowance provided on the table.

Since I did not eat at school and was given a bottle of hot tea, I saved my daily allowance.

Experiences in primary school are a time filled with various colorful memories.

It marks the beginning of our educational journey, form the foundation for further learning.

Here, we learn not only in the classroom but also through interactions with peers and experiences outside the classroom.

One of the most meaningful memories might be making new friends.

Primary school is a period where we begin to learn about the concept of friendship and how to build relationships with others.

Memories with friends playing together in the schoolyard or sharing lunch together are memories that remain ingrained in our minds.

Additionally, there are also engaging learning experiences. Perhaps we remember inspiring teachers, our favorite subjects, or our first successes in various fields.

Despite the challenges in learning, such as exams and assignments, they are experiences that develop our determination and patience.

Not to be overlooked are the sweet and humorous memories in the classroom. There might be moments when we shared jokes with friends or received surprises on our friends' birthdays.

These memories bring laughter and joy that add color to our primary school experience.

However, apart from the cheerful memories, there are also challenges and sad experiences.

There might be conflicts with classmates or failures in something we tried to achieve.

These experiences teach us about regret, concern, and how to rise again after failure.

Overall, experiences in primary school are an important starting point in our lives.

It is a time when we begin to form our identities, pursue dreams, and learn about ourselves and the world around us.

These memories carry valuable lessons that we will share and remember throughout our lives.

3) HEAD PREFECT

During a study session, there was a sudden announcement over school's loudspeaker.

All prefects were asked to gather in the school library.

The purpose was to announce the new Head Prefect. Several names were mentioned for the position, including me.

Finally, my name was announced as the Head Prefect of Raja Bahar National School in 1998.

I don't remember much about the duties of the Head Prefect.

At that time, I was mainly tasked with hosting school assemblies and reciting the morning prayer before classes' start and before leaving school. It was a valuable experience.

Being the emcee for school assemblies almost every week helped me overcome nervousness and gave me a bit of courage.

4) 5A

On the day the UPSR results were released, I rushed to school to see my examination result. When I arrived at the school gate, someone shouted towards me!

"Ali, you got 5A! Ali, you got 5A!" It was my good friend, Firdaus excited to be the first person who deliver that good news to me. He got 4A.

A smile was etched on my lips. I laughed joyfully in my heart.

The six years of sacrifice in primary school had paid off. The year-long dedication during Sixth Grade had borne fruit.

From early morning until midnight, all my focus was on UPSR.

My parents and siblings were proud. I was the only one among my siblings to achieve all A's in UPSR.

It was a source of pride for my parents. UPSR 5A.
Head Prefect.
Model Student Award.
School assembly emcee.

But, I am the only one among my eight siblings who never completed my education.

I only managed to hold a scroll during my kindergarten.
That is because there was a picture. Otherwise, I would not remember that moment.

That was the memory of my primary school days. Beautiful, isn't it? I am sure everyone has fond memories of their childhood.

A time when responsibilities and problems were not a concern. The sky was not always clear.

There were cloudy days, followed by rain that soaked the earth.

Sometimes, there was a gentle drizzle, sometimes a heavy downpour.

If it was monsoon season, the rain poured relentlessly, unsettling nature.

That is the cycle of nature. Likewise, the cycle of life. There are ups and downs.

Trials come one after another.

TIMELINE: 1999-2004

5) DOWN AND DROP

In 1999, I stepped into boarding school as my secondary school.

Marking a new episode in my life. My first day at school, I met new friends.

I became friendly with seniors. In the first week, seniors were already coming to the dorm to tell stories.

What stories? Ghost stories. Japanese soldiers lining up in the back corridor of the dorm.

Japanese soldiers dressed in brown, saluting fiercely. Can you imagine?

Then there were stories of "toyol" bathing in the swimming pool. "Toyol" stealing coins. If you want to know, "Toyol" is the smaller green guy with the scary face.

I felt alienating. Everything was new. Living independently.

Washing our own clothes. Following dormitory rules. Meal times, prayers, studying, sports, and sleep. Everything was systematic.

I tried to consider my academic performance as normal for the transitional year.

But apparently, it was not. My friends noticed a change or difference in me.

They said I was not like how I described myself during my primary school days. UPSR 5A, Head Prefect, but the reality back then was the opposite.

I became rebellious. My studies were unfocused. I did not understand what the teachers were teaching.

"Stupid and ignorant". Complete. It turns out that was a symptom of bipolar disorder, and I didn't realize it at the time.

I was still a teenager then, how would I have known? The symptoms just hit me without warning.

Experiences in secondary school are a time filled with various intriguing memories. It is a phase where we begin to step into adolescence and undergo significant changes in our lives.

Here, we face new challenges, expand our social circles, and deepen our understanding of ourselves.

One of the most prominent aspects of the secondary school experience is the development of social relationships.

We may encounter new friends, join different groups or clubs, and perhaps even experience our first romantic relationships.

All of these contribute to the development of our social and emotional skills.

Aside from the social aspect, academic experiences are also crucial.

In secondary school, academic pressures may increase with the higher level of difficulty in subjects and the demand for excellence.

We may experience both success and failure in various fields, but all of these are learning experiences that build our resilience and perseverance.

Furthermore, experiences outside the classroom also have a significant impact.

Extracurricular activities such as sports, clubs, or volunteer work provide opportunities to develop talents, leadership skills, and values like teamwork and team spirit.

However, as in every phase of life, there are also challenges and difficulties.

We may face pressure from various sources, including peers, teachers, or family. We may encounter social conflicts, concerns about the future, or difficulties in coping with academic pressure.

Overall, the secondary school experience is a unique and valuable journey.

It shapes who we become as adults, taking us through various experiences and tests that help us grow and mature.

Despite the challenges and difficulties, these experiences are also filled with joy, friendship, and proud achievements that will be remembered throughout our lifetime.

6) BIPOLAR SYMPTOMS

Bipolar disorder is a mental health condition characterized by extreme mood swings that include emotional highs (mania or hypomania) and lows (depression).

These mood swings can affect sleep, energy levels, judgment, behavior, and the ability to think clearly.

Here are some symptoms commonly associated with Bipolar disorder:

1. **Manic Episode Symptoms**:

   - Feeling unusually elated, euphoric, or irritable

   - Having a heightened sense of self-esteem or grandiosity

   - Increased energy levels and activity

   - Racing thoughts and rapid speech

   - Impulsivity and engaging in risky behaviors like excessive spending, reckless driving, or substance abuse

   - Decreased need for sleep

   - Difficulty concentrating or focusing on tasks

   - Unrealistic beliefs in one's abilities or powers

2. **Hypomanic Episode Symptoms**:

- Similar symptoms to manic episodes but less severe

- Generally, hypomania does not cause significant problems in social or work functioning

- Episodes may be perceived as periods of increased productivity or creativity

3. **Depressive Episode Symptoms**:

- Feeling sad, hopeless, or empty for a majority of the day

- Loss of interest or pleasure in activities once enjoyed

- Changes in appetite or weight (significant weight loss or gain)

- Insomnia or excessive sleeping

- Fatigue or loss of energy

- Feelings of worthlessness or excessive guilt

- Difficulty concentrating, making decisions, or remembering things

- Thoughts of death or suicide, suicide attempts, or self-harming behaviors

It is important to note that the severity and frequency of mood swings can vary from person to person.

Some individuals may experience more frequent and severe episodes, while others may have longer periods of stability between episodes.

If you or someone you know is experiencing symptoms of Bipolar disorder, it is crucial to seek help from a mental health professional.

Bipolar disorder is a treatable condition, and with proper diagnosis and management, individuals can lead fulfilling lives.

Treatment typically involves a combination of medication, psychotherapy, and lifestyle changes.

Early intervention can significantly improve outcomes and quality of life for individuals with Bipolar disorder.

Throughout my schooling, it was evident that I experienced symptoms of Bipolar disorder.

MANIA

1. Rapid and frequent changes of topic when speaking.

2. Easily angered.

3. Reduced need for sleep.

4. Racing thoughts.

5. Overflowing ideas.

6. Unsafe behavior.

7. Extravagance.

8.

DEPRESSION

1. Extreme sadness.

2. Always tired.

3. Lack of emotions.

4. Disinterest in everything.

5. Excessive sleep.

6. Super sensitivity.

Most of my story revolves around my secondary school years because Bipolar symptoms were very noticeable during this time.

Why? Typically, Bipolar symptoms strike individuals during early adolescence to early adulthood.

This time is critical for one's development. Identity crisis are common.

Even a slight mistake during this age can lead to lifelong repercussions. Pay close attention to your child at this age.

Watch out for any abnormalities. From childhood through adolescence to adulthood, sensitivity varies.

Bipolar is quite challenging to detect because patients usually behave normally and appear happy. It is considered a positive trait, masking the real issues.

In reality, patients face emotional difficulties that fluctuate and recur.

Neither the people around nor the patients themselves are aware. That is the danger.

That is why I dare to share a bit of my experience for public awareness.

Honestly, I would rather keep silent and avoid appearing in public, let alone sharing this experience.

The problems that arise from Bipolar symptoms are making me feel like to runaway from everyone around me.

Feeling worthless. Troubling others. All sorts of sad feelings. Sometimes, I just want to sleep and never wake up.

7) MANIA PHASE

Bipolar disorder is a condition where an individual experiences mood swings between mania and depression.

Hence, the name Bipolar. 'Polar' means poles. Bipolar means having two poles.

The two poles in this disorder refer to the feelings of mania and depression.

The mood cycles of Bipolar disorder can be rapid.

Within the same week, a Bipolar patient's mood can fluctuate between depression and mania.

However, most Bipolar patients have a slow cycle. This means that they will experience a state of mania for weeks or months before switching to a state of depression or vice versa.

My experience during the manic phase:

1. **Rapid and frequent changes of topic when speaking.**

   Speaking quickly and unclearly. It is difficult to grasp the details. Have you ever experienced it?

   For example:

   Friend: Have you finished reading the book?

   *Me: ! @%$^&&***()% bla..bla... not yet (I'm not done yet. I don't even remember a word of it yet.)*

   Meaning the details are unclear. Perhaps only the last word can be understood.

   While speaking, the brain is busy thinking and other ideas come, causing the patient to easily switch to another topic.

   Before finishing the topic being discussed, they jump to another topic as if they want to convey many things at once.

   The mind is constantly scripting without pause.
   Oh, my head is pounding. Even the listeners feel dizzy.

2. **Easily angered: Angry. Quick-tempered.**

Normal, right? It is normal for normal people because it will neutralize. Angry for a moment, then okay.

But for Bipolar sufferers, the anger lasts. One outburst of anger will become worse and continue until the emotions stabilize again.

For example: Driving a car, suddenly someone honks. A sudden feeling of anger arises, bubbling in the stomach.

We honk back at the person. We curse. Maybe we hit the person's car.

Maybe we have a big fight. Maybe we hit them until death.

Yes, it can reach that point because emotions are already in turmoil.

The mind cannot think rationally. Is it over? No.

Waves of dissatisfaction continue to surge in the mind. It will continue to play in the mind.

Maybe for a few hours. Maybe for a few days. A week. Depending on the severity and medication.

I also cannot stand the sound of firecrackers. I still remember I kicked my own brother who played with firecrackers.

That is why this disorder is very dangerous if not treated early.

Risk to oneself and others.

It is quite unfortunate that I was diagnosed after years of suffering.

After various bad things happened in my life. After I swallowed all the insults and slander.

Finally, I came to the psychiatrist myself. I am not crazy.

But I feel something was wrong with me. I take mood stabilizer medication.

It helps reduce the more severe effects. Although it does not fully help, but it is better than no treatment at all.

3. **Reduced need for sleep.**

When in a manic mood, I sleep less. Even if I try to sleep, I do not feel sleepy.

Even if I sleep late, I can wake up early. What's more, I wander around the dormitory area.

Visiting classmates' dorms. Going from one dorm to another. One dorm can accommodate about 10 people.

They become victims of my mischief. They have to listen to my talk.

Sometimes I preach. Sometimes I lecture.

Some of my friends said I would become a lawyer. Some predicted I would become a politician.

Even though I was really tired when I talked non-stop.

But my brain pushed me to keep talking and entertaining my friends.

4. **Very Bad Thoughts.**

How bad is it? It is hard to explain. If we follow existing cases, there are those who even claim to be Prophet Isa (Jesus).

Making various claims. But I have not come across anyone claiming to be Superman's twin yet.

Some even become fortune tellers, predicting the future.
When the mind is unstable, whatever is being thought is not normal.

Sometimes it is downright embarrassing. But indeed, it is shameful.

That is why we do not dare to come forward. Especially not to expose our own shame.

The mental health stigma still persists in society. Even though mental illness cases are increasing every year.

Perhaps those who mock mental patients eventually get afflicted themselves.

This illness strikes silently. Do not think we are immune to this attack.

Take care of your mental health. Sometimes we are in abnormal conditions.

Understand our conditions that are beyond our control.
We did not ask to be this way.

We hope for sympathy and empathy, not ridicule and insults.

Personally, I dare not reveal the very severe thoughts I experience. Let it remain a secret. Want to know more? You cannot.

5. **Overflowing Ideas**

When the chemical balance in the brain is unstable, the mind becomes overly active.

Ideas flow incessantly and cannot be restrained. These ideas can be either good or bad. It is like a script being formed endlessly.

The ideas can be grand and sometimes illogical.

I once had the idea to write about materialistic imagination.

I envisioned myself as the CEO of a bank and a conglomerate company, holding significant positions in the corporate and banking world.

I have an interest in economics and investment.

During my primary school, I enjoyed watching economic news, especially foreign currency exchange.

My imagination in the economic world is excessive.

It is like being transported into a fantasy dream.

If the idea is logical, it can be implemented. Sometimes when it comes, it is enjoyable to indulge while snacking on sunflower seeds.

The downside is when it arrives, I have to stop whatever else I am doing and attend to it first.

Sometimes it feels like talking to myself. When situations like this arise, I find joy in working.

There is excessive and active energy. Want to experience it? Let's switch brains for a moment.

6. **Unsafe Behavior**

People might just think it is mischievous. Mischievousness is indeed normal.

I was quite well-behaved in primary school. Head prefect, prayer leader, how mischievous could I be?

I once pinched my friend in class until he got angry, then he pinched me back.

He was quite bigger than me. So the force of his pinch startled me.

I had silent. Realized the mischief. My friend said I once ran on the second-floor dormitory balcony.

How could I forget this moment? But that was an unsafe behavior I once engaged in.

The dormitory building has two floors. I ran on the second-floor balcony.

If I fell, I could break my leg. But at that moment, I did not think about anything dangerous that I will face during that time if it is happening.

I also liked climbing the flagpole. It was satisfying when I managed to climb it. The flagpole swayed easily.

Can you believe it?

"Here! The proof captured by my broken camera when I am climbing the flagpole. Luckily, I am slim and lightweight."

I also accidentally cycle a distance of 40km, from my house to my friend's house.

The initial ride was just for fun, but somehow the idea came to continue cycling all the way to my friend's house.

When I arrived at his house, he was extremely surprised.

It was as if an uninvited guest had arrived.

The most surprised person was my mother when I called her and told her that I was already at my friend's house.

I had to stay over at his place. Since I was already there, we engaged in some activities together.

Instead of just the two of us, we then went to another friend's house, making it three of us now.

7. **Extravagance**

Spending excessively without restraint. Money that is available will be spent and not saved.

Almost every week, my parents would come to visit and give me pocket money.

I would spend that money until it runs out. I often spend on friends as well, to the point where they think I come from a wealthy background.

This extravagant spending isn't very noticeable at the moment due to limited finances.

I may seem well-off because I'm given pocket money that exceeds my needs.

I'm a spoiled child. There was one time when I stuck money in a locker, something I never did before.

These are some symptoms when in a manic mood.

8) DEPRESSION PHASE

1. Ultra Stress

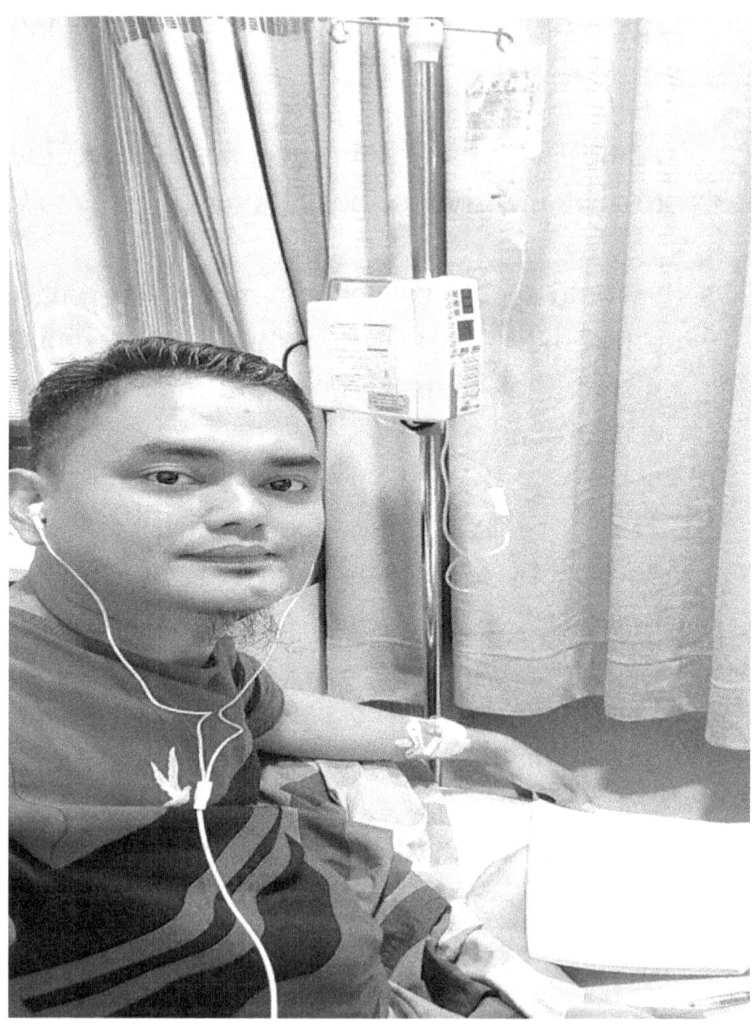

When this note was drafted, I found myself admitted to the hospital. It took me a year to complete the manuscript of the life story of a Bipolar Fighter.

I would write in the book, then type it out, and then edit it. Adding what was necessary, deleting what was not, and then editing again... it was quite stressful.

My hope is that readers can derive some useful benefit from this small piece of my life story, which may not be much.

I have became a diabetes patient since 2013, that was over 10 years ago.

Stress is one of the causes of diabetes besides diet.

Stress is the thing I want to avoid the most because this emotional imbalance leads to other bad things. Worst of all, suicide.

"Ultra Stress" is the term I use to explain my condition.

It does not need a specific reason to stress. When the mood turns depressive, stress will suddenly come. No need for a reason.

Strange, isn't it? That is the difference between the stress of a mental patient and a normal person.

Normal people get stressed under pressure. Normal people, when stressed, can calm down in various ways.

Mental patients, when stressed, medication is the answer.

Because the cause of stress is due to chemical imbalance in the brain and it takes time to stabilize.

When in the depression phase, do not fights with patient.

No matter how bad the stress of a normal person is, the stress of a mental patient is worse than that.

Learn how to handle mental patients. Empathize with them. Okay?

2. **Constant Fatigue**

During the depression phase, everything seems bleak.

Life becomes exhausting. Extremely tired. Once, while I was eating alone in the kitchen, my plate suddenly fell and broke.

It was because of extreme fatigue. Even eating feels exhausting.

But I still have to eat as an effort to feel full and energized.

I'm too tired even to cry. Even after sleeping for a long time, waking up still feels tired.

I sleep again. Luckily, I manage to wake up again.

3. **Emotionless**

Empty. No emotions. It is emptiness in emotions, not in the spirit.

Empty because of the imbalance of fluids in the brain that signals 'empty' to the mind.

The emptiness feels like watching a comedy but not laughing.

Asking and answering monosyllabically. If hungry, go eat alone.

Until now, I have not played any games. So, the snake game serves to fill the void during my emptiness.

How long? It could be a few days. A week. Two weeks. The effects are very noticeable to me and those around me.

Reading? I can do it for a while. Then lost focus. But somehow it helps when reading something what we interested in.

When feeling empty, nothing seems to work. Things that are usually done get stuck. Things we are interested in doing also become interrupted. That is how it goes.

4. **Lack of Interest in Everything**

When depressed, everything seems to lose its appeal.

Things that we used to enjoy doing are now hindered.

Even activities we used to be passionate about become uninteresting. For instance, I enjoy reading.

I love reading Dr. Tuah's books, whether they are motivational books or novels.

These books have greatly helped me find inspiration in life.

However, when my mood swings towards depression comes, I do not have the energy to read.

Life feels empty. There are plenty of things I could do, but I have no desire to do them.

5. **Excessive Sleeping**

During depression phase, all I want to do are sleep throughout the day.

Because when I am awake, my brain does not function properly.

I feel like getting angry, everything feels chaotic, sad, and all sorts of unpleasant feelings.

The only way to get rid of all of these feeling is by sleeping.

What I least want is taking forbidden substances to alleviate the discomfort during the depressive phase.

I hope I could stay away from that.

6. **Super Sensitivity**

People say I'm easily torn apart. And it's true.

Don't mess around with mental illness. If emotions are unstable, the mind is easily shattered.

Very sensitive to the environment. If someone talks in front of them, they think the person is gossiping about them.

Sometimes, what people say may be interpreted differently.

Don't be too sarcastic with mental illness sufferers.

But don't be too blunt either. Find a middle ground.

9) MALAYSIAN CERTIFICATE OF EDUCATION (MCE)

I maximized my energy for the SPM (Sijil Pelajaran Malaysia - Malaysian Certificate of Education). I focused during study sessions.

When I returned home, I rested properly. Only at night I have the strength to revise my lessons.

"Congratulations, 7A," I received SMS (message) from my Mathematics teacher who also supervised the SPM.

As expected, the results I obtained were within expectations.

I always set my own expectations so I would not be surprised by my actual results.

I am not used to accept the surprise. It would distract my mind.

I got 7A, 1B, 1C, 1D, 1E., I have all the letters except F. That's fair, right?

LEMBAGA PEPERIKSAAN MALAYSIA
MALAYSIAN EXAMINATIONS SYNDICATE

Calon yang tersebut namanya di bawah telah mengambil
Peperiksaan Sijil Pelajaran Malaysia dan berkelayakan menerima

SIJIL PELAJARAN MALAYSIA

Calon ini telah mencapai kelulusan seperti yang tercatat di bawah
bagi mata pelajaran berkenaan.

NIK NOOR AZLIE B RAJA SEMAN   860324-29-   DA032A028

SEK MEN KEB RAJA SAKTI KOTA BHARU KELANTAN

Mata Pelajaran [Subject]	Peringkat [Grade]
BAHASA MELAYU	1A (SATU)
BAHASA INGGERIS	6C (ENAM)
PENDIDIKAN ISLAM	1A (SATU)
SEJARAH	1A (SATU)
MATEMATIK	1A (SATU)
SAINS	2A (DUA)
MATEMATIK TAMBAHAN	8E (LAPAN)
PRINSIP PERAKAUNAN	4B (EMPAT)
TASAWWUR ISLAM	1A (SATU)
PENDIDIKAN AL-QURAN & AS-SUNNAH	2A (DUA)
BAHASA ARAB (KOMUNIKASI)	7D (TUJUH)

JUMLAH MATAPELAJARAN SEBELAS
PEPERIKSAAN TAHUN 2004

041129135

AA 0047244

[Sila lihat sebelah]

Pengarah Peperiksaan
[Director of Examinations]
Kementerian Pelajaran Malaysia
[Ministry of Education Malaysia]

TIMELINE: 2005-2009

10) UNIVERSITI TEKNOLOGI MARA (UiTM)

I have received an offer to continued my study in Diploma in Accounting at UiTM Machang, Kelantan, Malaysia.

Began from here, the symptoms of Bipolar disorder peaked.

Manic and depressive episodes switched on and off. In my secondary school, the medium of instruction was Malay.

Nevertheless, at here, everything was in English. Even though I had a C6 in English, it was just only pass for my exam.

All subjects were taught in English. I tried to adapt to the new environment.

Accounting was not new to me. But when taught in English, I was shocked.

It seemed like I had never studied Accounting before.

My friends noticed that I liked to talk and sometimes my speech was not clear during manic episodes.

When depressed, I would become more silent.

I joined the Debate Club. Ironically, I never actually debated. Just for the experience.

I spent my first semester participating in Debate Club activities, Speeches, and the Islamic Association.

We organized several major events, which earned me a few certificates.

UNIVERSITI TEKNOLOGI MARA
CAWANGAN KELANTAN

Sijil Penghargaan

Bahawasanya UiTM Cawangan Kelantan
Dengan penuh rasa bangga dan sukacitanya
menganugerahkan sijil penghargaan ini
kepada

NIK NOOR AZLIE BIN RAJA SEMAN
860324

Kerana
jasa dan khidmat bakti
beliau yang cemerlang sebagai

PENGACARA MAJLIS

FORUM REMAJA
Sempena Festival Kolej (FESKO)
09 Mac 2006

Timbalan Pengarah Kampus
Hal Ehwal Pelajar

At the peak of my manic episode, as an introvert, I hosted the Youth Forum event in three languages: Malay, Arabic, and English.

I successfully managed the night event. I do not know where that courage came from.

It turned out that was the manic mood. I felt energized to make it successful.

I started to be known from the top management to the bottom levels.

After the program, I had the opportunity to dine with the Director of UiTM. Many students began to recognize me.

However, my academic performance continued to decline.

I had to be absent from classes and even exams due to extreme fatigue. So many classes that I missed, and there were exams where I did not show up.

When the results came out, my grade point average was quite low.

Low enough to be considered for dismissal. I surrendered myself to the situation. It was not my place here.

But strangely, I was given another chance to continue my second semester.

So, what happened in my second semester? Not much changed.

I still struggled to grasp the subjects, all subjects were taught in English.

I was still tired. Stressed. Unable to focus in my studies.

Finally, the semester results were released. My grade point average was still low that lead me to my actual dismissal.

Thus, my episode at UiTM came to an end. Goodbye, UiTM.

11) FORM 6 (STPM)

My next attempt was to take the Malaysian Higher School Certificate (STPM) at a private school in my town.

I studied formally for 4 months. I lost focus again. It was boring.

However, I enjoyed studying the General Studies subject.

Learning about the separation of Executive and Legislative powers, as well as Legislation.

Nevertheless, in real life, it was not quite like that. Due to boredom and losing focus on studying, I made the decision to move to Kuala Lumpur.

MAJLIS PEPERIKSAAN MALAYSIA
(MALAYSIAN EXAMINATIONS COUNCIL)

SIJIL TINGGI PERSEKOLAHAN MALAYSIA
(MALAYSIA HIGHER SCHOOL CERTIFICATE)

Adalah disahkan bahawa **NIK NOOR AZLIE B RAJA SEMAN**
(This is to certify that

No. Kad Pengenalan   860324-29-   telah menduduki peperiksaan SIJIL TINGGI
Identity Card No.   *has sat for the Malaysia Higher School*

PERSEKOLAHAN MALAYSIA dan telah mencapai gred kelulusan seperti yang tercatat bagi
Certificate examination and reached the grade of pass specified in each of the following

mata pelajaran yang tersebut di bawah ini:
subjects.)

Angka Giliran: **SB105/3024**   Tahun Peperiksaan: **2009**
(Index No.)   *(Year of Examination)*

Mata Pelajaran *(Subject)*	Gred *(Grade)*	NGMP* *(SGP)*	
PENGAJIAN AM	B+	3.33	(LULUS PENUH)
BAHASA MALAYSIA	A-	3.67	(LULUS PENUH)
SEJARAH	C+	2.33	(LULUS PENUH)
GEOGRAFI	C+	2.33	(LULUS PENUH)

Bilangan Mata Pelajaran Lulus: **4**   *Nilai Gred Mata Pelajaran
(Number of Subjects Passed)   *(Subject Grade Point)*

Prof Tan Sri Dato' Dzulkifli bin Abdul Razak   **Omar bin Abu Bakar**
Pengerusi   Ketua Eksekutif
(Chairman)   *(Chief Executive)*
Majlis Peperiksaan Malaysia   Majlis Peperiksaan Malaysia
(Malaysian Examinations Council)   *(Malaysian Examinations Council)*

AD 015158

05030/09   Sila lihat sebelah
                                       (P.T.O.)

TIMELINE: 2010-2012

WORKING

12) CARREFOUR

In Kuala Lumpur, I lived with my sister and her family. I applied for various jobs that were suitable for my qualifications.

I applied for a sales assistant position at Carrefour Mid-Valley. I started working immediately.
Standing at the cashier's counter for 4 hours without rest because too many customers come and go.

I just got a short break for prayer and a foot massage. Then, I got back to work.

It was very exhausting. There was no time to sit even for a moment. Although I was careful with customer transactions, there were still a few ringgit discrepancies.

After a week, I submitted my resignation letter. I could not stand non-stop for 4 to 5 hours at the cashier's counter every day.

It is not that I could not sit, but I did not have time to sit because customers were always lining up to pay for the goods they purchased.

13) UNIVERSITI TEKNOLOGI MALAYSIA (UTM) KUALA LUMPUR

The day after resigning, I received a call from UTM KL. They said there was an immediate interview.

The next day, I went there with my brother-in-law. The administration's management interviewed me.

They said there was a clerk job in a new department that needed to be filled urgently.

However, the job offered was on a part-time basis. I accepted it with an open heart because it was much better than standing for hours at the counter.

At least, it was a new experience for me in the working world. Since I had no experience with clerical work in government department, I had to fumble my way through starting this job.

After working at UTM KL for a year, I resigned. This is because I wanted to continue my studies again.

I have enrolled on a professional accounting course, Certified Accounting Technician (CAT) under the Association of Chartered Certified Accountants (ACCA), at the Baitulmal Professional Institute (IPB).

My interest in Accounting was still strong. I enjoyed counting money.

I pretended to study again. My father even bought me a new motorcycle to continue my studies.

But as usual, I only lasted for one semester. My ability to focus was very low.

I did not understand anything that I learnt. My dream of continuing my studies was dashed. Study.

Stop halfway. Study again. Stop again. Exhausted. Sad. Disappointed. The tests did not stop here.

14) DIABETES

I complained to the doctor when I felt extreme fatigue. After an examination, my blood sugar level was checked.

That was the first time my blood sugar level was checked.

I was diagnosed with diabetes when the blood glucose meter reading was 25 mmol/L.

I was 26 years old at that time. I was extremely shocked.

Thus began the era of insulin injections into my belly. Sometimes into my thighs. It was torture.

When injected into the belly multiple times, the muscles would stiffen and become resistant to the injections.

I had to inject in other places as well. I had to inject twice a day. Can you imagine?

Moral of the story, take care of your health from a young age. We cannot predict our future. We can only try to avoid disasters, but if they are destined to happen, then we should be patient.

Diabetes, also known as "kencing manis" in Malay, is a disease involving high levels of blood glucose in the body.

This occurs when the body either cannot produce enough insulin or cannot effectively use the insulin it produces, which is necessary to control blood glucose levels.

There are two main types of diabetes:
1. **Type 1 Diabetes**: Typically begins in children or young adults. This occurs when the body's immune system attacks and damages the insulin-producing cells in the pancreas. Individuals with type 1 diabetes require insulin injections to control their blood sugar levels.

2. **Type 2 Diabetes**: More commonly occurring and often associated with an unhealthy lifestyle, such as an unbalanced diet and lack of physical activity. Initially, the body still produces insulin but not enough or it is not effective. In most cases, type 2 diabetes can be managed through healthy eating, regular exercise, and in some cases, medications.

Symptoms of diabetes include constant thirst, frequent urination, unexpected weight loss, fatigue, and blurred vision.

Diabetes management involves monitoring blood glucose levels, healthy eating, regular exercise, and taking medications if necessary.

Uncontrolled diabetes can lead to serious complications such as heart problems, eye problems, and nerve disorders.

Therefore, it is important to seek treatment and adopt a healthy lifestyle for individuals with diabetes.

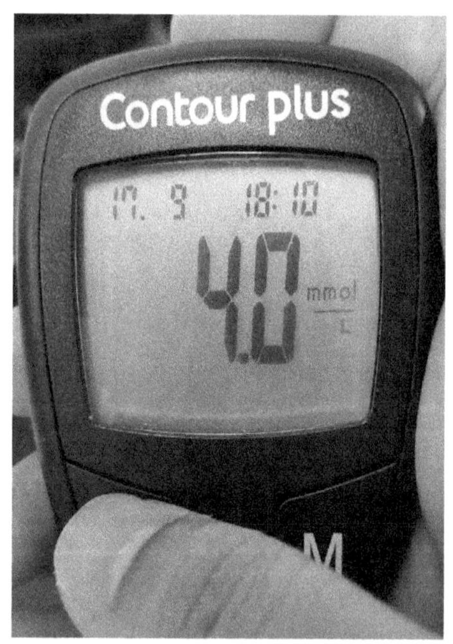

This is a normal blood sugar reading. Maintain this reading for long-term health.

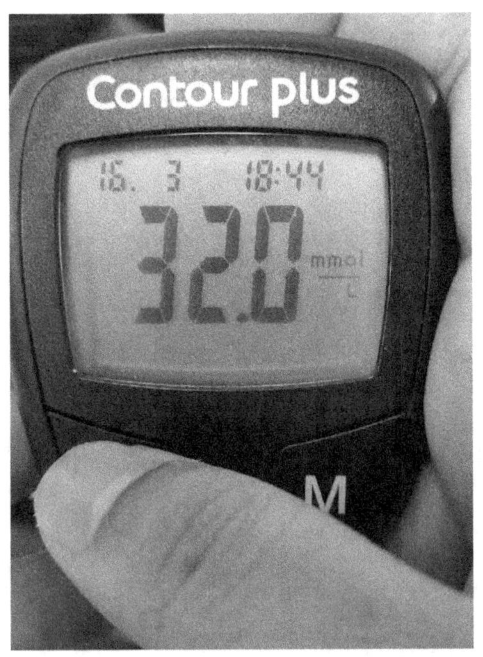

This is a very high blood sugar reading. If your blood sugar level reaches this level, you should seek emergency medical attention as it could bring you to death.

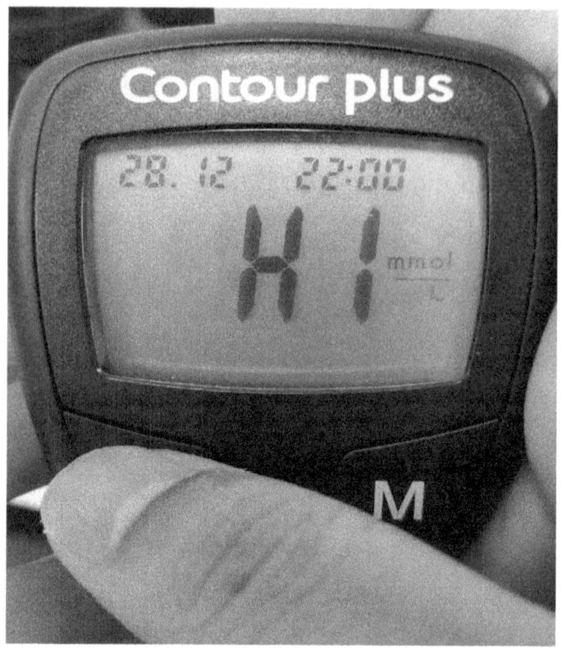

This is an extremely high blood sugar level where the meter cannot read. I am familiar with meter reading like this, especially when I miss my insulin injections.

15) INLAND REVENUE BOARD MALAYSIA (IRBM)

Study, then quit, then work, then quit, and study again, followed by dismissal.

I applied for a job through Jobs Malaysia. Among the positions I applied for was at IRBM.

Six months later, while I was sweeping rubbish in the backyard of my village house, I received an interview letter from IRBM in Cyberjaya, Malaysia.

They had interviewed 100 people at that time, even though there were only 10 vacancies advertised.

With confidence, I successfully managed the interview. It was similar to anticipating the results of my SPM exams beforehand, just as with this interview.

Because I could not deal with any surprises. Six months later, while still sweeping rubbish, my sister informed me that there was a job offer as an Administrative Assistant (Accounting) at IRBM.

I headed to KL with joy because I got a permanent job in a statutory body. My heart was filled with joy about this job offer. It provided me with a new experience.

In reality, my fate has become worsened. I worked for 6 months before I decided to resign within 24 hours.

Problems kept piling up, it was like I had fallen down stairs, then was hit by a falling tree, and finally struck by a wild boar.

That is the imagery. I cried endlessly in front of my Head of Department while requesting to resign.

If only I had known I had Bipolar Type 2 mental illness, I would have tried to control the problems that arose, whether intentionally or unintentionally.

But alas, the damage was done. I resigned within 24 hours. I could not bear to continue working anymore.

Reading about some symptoms of Bipolar disorder includes excessive spending.

That is what I faced without knowing the real cause. At that time, I was severely scolded due to my actions. It seemed to happen in the blink of eyes.

Within a month, I lost hundreds of thousands because I got involved in get-rich-quick schemes.

I did not think further. The desire to get rich quickly has trapped me. The pressure to get married added to the urgency to gather money.

I borrowed money here and there to settle my tight monthly commitments.

Digging one hole to fill another, eventually my debts increased.

I wake up every morning thinking about debts. My mind was in turmoil.

During that time, I rented a place near my workplace alone.

Can you imagine being alone with debt as high as a mountain ready to crush you? No, right?

Every morning before going to work, I cried in the storeroom. The stress was unbearable. Dealing with people every day was exhausting.

Finally, I could not bear to think about the problems that kept piling up.

I submitted a resignation letter within 24 hours. I could not work anymore.

Plus, the new team-oriented work culture was quite awkward for me.

I rarely communicated with other staff unless absolutely necessary.

Until there was a Hari Raya celebration, I had to attend and felt out of place because I did not know anyone except my colleagues from same department.

I felt pressure thinking about what people thought about me.

Overthinking. I came to work, focused on getting work done, and left as soon as it was time to go home.

The decision was final. I resigned with a 24-hour notice. I had to pay one month's salary to the employer.

16) SELLING HONEY

My last endeavor in KL was selling honey with my partner. Yemeni Sidr Honey. The best honey in the world.

Then, I colluded with my partner to import honey from Yemen and sell it through Facebook ads.

During that time, Facebook ads were still new (2013), and running ads for a short while would immediately generate sales.

However, this business did not last long. I was enthusiastic at first, but gradually lost interest.

I did not expect it. But that is a symptom of bipolar disorder.

When manic, I want to do everything. When depressed, nothing seems to work out.

If possible, I just want to sleep and not wake up.

17) RETURNING TO HOMETOWN

After everything fell apart in the capital city, I returned to my hometown.

I did not know what to do. Mentally shattered. It got worse when I still did not know that I had a mental illness.

Physically exhausted, attacked by diabetes. There were times when I did not inject insulin for months. My legs were always numb. My fingers were trembling like Parkinson's.

When I went back to my hometown, there was nothing to do.

I became very quiet. My parents did not say anything. They did not ask me to do anything.

Whether they were sad about my situation or did not want to bother me, I did not know.

I had not thought about seeing a psychiatrist. I was afraid of being called crazy... haha.

My daily routine was just sitting in my room like a trapped goat. I still did not miss my prayers.
After Fajr, I would sleep. Wake up at Dhuhr, bathe, and eat.

I could not sleep because the room felt like a sauna from the heat of the sun.

Even if I slept, it felt like being roasted like a goat. In the late afternoon, I would sweep the trash and burn it.

At night, I would stare at my phone. For months, I sat in my room.

No motivation to live or rise from failure. It was painful to face solitude.

If I did not understand what was happening to me, how could anyone else.

18) WORKING IN SINGAPORE

My worst problem at that time was being burdened
by mountain of debt.

I was pressured to work again to solve the debt
issues related to my family.

It is somewhat private to share here because it
involves family, but it was the reality I had to face.

With severe diabetes, a shattered mental state, my
brain could only think of making money with
limited energy.

I decided to work in Singapore, with the theory that
the pay that I can get is higher than in Malaysia.

It was my first time went to Singapore. I did not
know what awaited me there.

But my heart was determined to make money to pay
off the debt. I met the employer's representative to
be brought into Singapore.

Walking across the border checkpoint was quite
exhausting.

Upon reaching the Singapore side, I exchanged
Malaysian Ringgit for Singapore Dollars.

Arriving at the workplace, a hotel in Geylang, I was briefed and given hotel attire.

Thus, began my new job as a Housekeeper. From a permanent clerk to a hotel Housekeeper.

Work started at 7 in the morning. Cleaning hotel rooms. Changing sheets and pillowcases.

I had to learn how to change sheets for days. There was a target number of rooms to be cleaned every day.

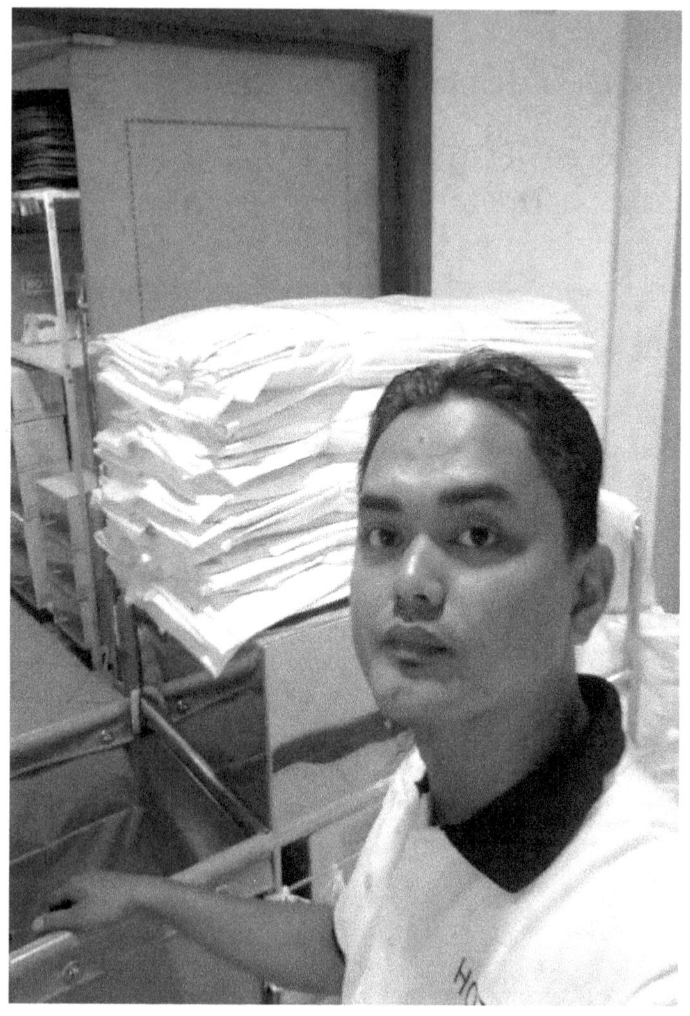

The morning routine involves filling the trolley with room sets such as bed sheets, towels, tissues, water bottles, and other items.

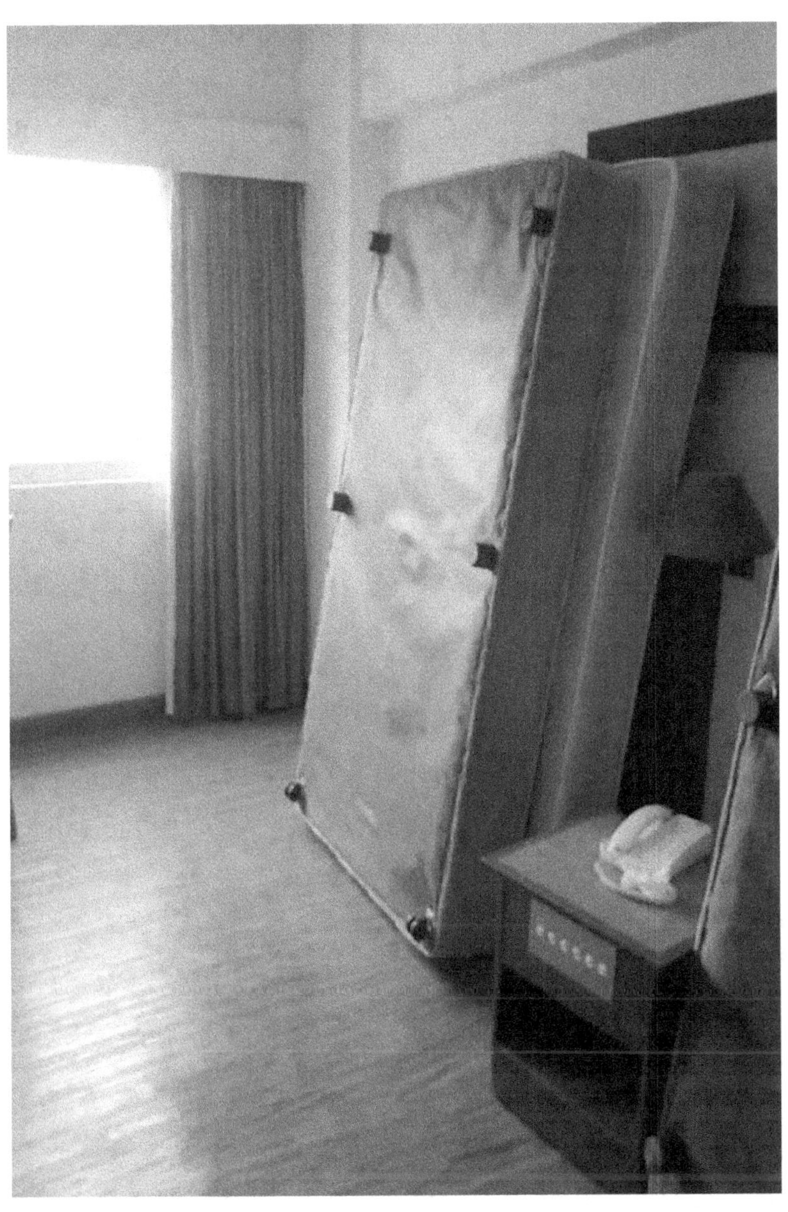

There are times when I have to do full cleaning. I have to lift up the double bed alone.

The used bed sheets and towels are collected here and then sent to the laundry center.

This is a complete set for the Housekeeper.

Tired until my white eyes turn yellow. My black eyes turn blue .

After working, I went to the food court to fill up my stomach.

Two weeks working as a housekeeper, I felt I could not bear it anymore.

With the help of my coworker, I was brought back to Malaysia. It turns out it was their habit to do job like that.

Not many people can endure working there. I was taken at night by the last bus to cross the Johor Causeway.

Let me continue a bit about working in Singapore. Actually, I came to work in Singapore twice.

A year later, I came to work in Singapore again. This time, I worked at a food court.

The challenge was even more tough than the first time. Working rotated shifts in several food courts.

After Fajr, I rushed to catch the bus. I need to arrive at the food court by 7 in the morning.

There were already many people in the morning. I had to clean tables, collect used plates, bowls, and cups to be placed in their respective areas.

What time did I finish work? 10 at night. Overtime? No, that was regular work, no overtime.

7 in the morning until 10 at night. 13 hours of non-stop working in a fasting state. Break time? None.

If you want to rest, hide for a while in the storage area, but not too long, the supervisor will come and check.

The supervisor and I were among the last to leave. It was because I did not know how to go back alone by bus.

Before going home, the supervisor would take a short break and chat with friends at the food court. Smoking and drinking beer without feeling guilty in front of me.

Going home by bus. Arriving home around 11 at night, thinking I could sleep immediately.

But there was another problem. The mosquitoes kept bothering my legs. I could not sleep that night. I was busy scratching my itchy legs, suddenly I had to get up and get ready for the daily routine.

We were placed in a ground-floor apartment, renting the living room and one bedroom. The other two bedrooms were used by the homeowners.

We squeezed in the living room. One more room was already full. The living conditions were mediocre. Just enough to sleep briefly.

Then wake up sweating half the day to get a handful of rice. How long did I work this time? One week.

19) TUBERCULOSIS

One day, I had a cough. Thought it was just a regular cough.

After a week, I went to the clinic. I had given cough medicine. The cough did not go away, in fact, it got worse.

A week later, I went to the hospital and was suspected of having dengue fever, but there were no signs of dengue fever.

A week later, I went to the clinic again. That morning the doctor asked me to have an x-ray.

A few hours later.

"The tuberculosis bacteria have attacked half of your lungs," said the doctor while pointing out the white spots on the x-ray indicating the bacteria.

Imagine that, coughing for a month only to find out I had tuberculosis.

Those who have had tuberculosis know how painful it is.

When coughing, it feels like all the organs in the chest want to come out. Preventing infectious diseases like tuberculosis is quite strict.

For the first month, I went back and forth to the clinic to take medication.

I had to take medication in front of the nurse. Then it was recorded in a small book.

What medication, what type, how many pills. I vomited at home because the medication did not suit me yet.

In the afternoon, I would definitely have a high fever. I only felt a bit relieved at night. That is how it was for several months.

Changed medication after a few months. Because I have diabetes, the medication that was supposed to be taken for 6 months was extended for another 3 months, making it 9 months.

So that year was the year of treating tuberculosis.

Going back and forth to the clinic until the nurse recognized me. Taking tuberculosis medication is like undergoing chemotherapy.

The medication attacks the bacteria and other cells simultaneously. My face turned black and became pale.

20) TOOTHACHE

Following my recovery from tuberculosis, I experienced toothache.

I hurried to the HUSM (Hospital Universiti Sains Malaysia) dentistry clinic. My tooth was extracted more quickly because there were dental medical students there.

I did not care if a medical student extracted it, as long as the toothache went away. Initially, I had to undergo an examination.

Then, we scheduled an appointment to have the tooth extracted. I was also scaling my teeth.

After several visits to HUSM, I felt compelled to see a psychiatrist (PSY).

I was apprehensive, but it did not hurt to try. Since I did not feel like I had a mental illness, I was hesitant.

Being crazy was not on my mind. However, why did it appear like everything went wrong in my life?

21) DIAGNOSED BIPOLAR

"Doctor, I think I should visit a psychiatrist. I have already tried traditional medicine. It does not seem to work. It is getting worse. I am unable to finish my studies. I work, then I quit. In Sixth Grade, I was a classmate of your cousin. But this is how it turned out". I told the doctor to get a referral letter.

I then received a referral letter from the doctor. I went to the PSY Clinic with that letter. They subsequently scheduled an appointment date with PSY.

I get anxious when the time to meet PSY comes. Apparently, many people meet the PSY at that time.

I was called by a doctor. She asked a few questions while flipping through a medical dictionary, maybe.

I answered calmly, there was a moment when I stopped because there was a sad part.

I was allowed to calm down for a while before continuing the Q&A. I told my story from primary school until I secluded myself at home.

About the symptoms during school and university. I told the doctor about my debts, almost everything I shared and there were some things I did not tell here because it was too private.

Then the doctor left. Maybe to refer to a PSY Specialist. A few minutes later, she came back.

"You are confirmed to have Bipolar Type 2," the doctor said to me. I am speechless.

Like what I expected, but I am still shocked. Life is full of surprises.
I was given mood stabilizers medicine and an appointment two weeks later.

The effect of the medicine is very noticeable. Emotions feel empty.

Feeling stupid too. If I take the medicine at night, I will feel sleepy again in the morning.

I have attended several appointments, and I am continuously taking Epilim Chrono medication. It is good to maintain a stable mood.

Want to know a story?

There was one session of PSY appointment made in an open room.

I could clearly see a female patient who was talking incessantly in front of the doctor.

Her facial expression was very excited to talk.

It reminded me of myself during school and university.
That was my condition during manic episodes. Talking non-stop with unclear details and fast.

Just like how I used to be. Then I bumped into her at the pharmacy counter.
After chatting, it turns out she also has Bipolar disorder.

Suffering from Bipolar disorder while at the Institute of Teacher Education , until she got a teaching position.

I do not remember whether she was dismissed as a teacher or have been given special leave. Her story was almost the same as mine, but slightly different.

If I underwent traditional treatment for years before referring to PSY. She underwent traditional treatment a year later and referred to PSY for years.

Bipolar disorder is a universal illness. We will not consider someone mentally ill until they admit it themselves.

I myself was well known during school and university.
So, what is the problem with mental patients, especially Bipolar?

The problem is that people assume I am healthy as it is.

But actually, I am struggling with unstable emotions. Depressing and manic.

Repeatedly until I feel exhausted. The problem is that many bad things happened in my life due to Bipolar disorder, but the blame is fully on me.

How many years have I endured? Imagine. From school, the initial symptoms started at the age of 14 (year 2000) until I was diagnosed at the age of 32 (year 2017).

17 years of suffering from Bipolar disorder without treatment or medication.

As a result, I did not know I had an illness, but I had to endure all its symptoms.

After being diagnosed, is that the end? No. I have to depend on medication forever.

The harm caused by this Bipolar disorder takes time to recover.

Many things were severely affected: lots of debts, relationships, the environment, and mental torment due to not being treated from the beginning.

22) BANKRUPTCY

One thing I wanted to avoid finally happened. One evening, a man from town came to see me.

He said he was a representative lawyer of the bank. I was given a letter to attend the bankruptcy judgment at the court.

I did not attend due to financial reasons. The proceedings continued anyway, and I was subsequently declared bankrupt.

My bank accounts have been frozen. I tried to pay my personal loan installments.
But over time, I ran out of money. My debts piled up.

Finally, I gave up. Being bankrupted is the last resort.

But I was given a chance to open a new bank account to make installment payments to the Malaysian Department of Insolvency (MdI). RM100 per month. I am struggling to pay this amount every month.

It is difficult for me to make people around me understand that I find it difficult to work.

I tried to work in Singapore. If I could work, why would I quit my job at a statutory body with a higher salary?

I tried to find a job. I once got a job at a furniture store.

The first day, I rode my motorcycle to work. Coming back at night, the motorcycle light broke.

I just continued my journey down the dark road. The second day of work, my boss asked me to see him.

He told me that I was not qualified to work as a laborer there. I was paid for two days of work. You are fired!

RISING AGAIN

23) WORKING AGAIN

After several years of seclusion in my village, I was invited to work in Kuala Lumpur.

My brother-in-law handles the sales for one of the housing projects. I tried. There is no harm in trying.

Even though I had to face the public. I must try. Thus, a new episode began in Kuala Lumpur.
I am selling houses. Learning to approach people to buy their own residences.

I learned to calculate loan eligibility, the difference in calculation methods for each bank, loan rates, and which bank offers the lowest and highest rates. MRTT and MLTT.

The commission is not bad either. Suitable for those who are extroverted, have excellent communication skills, and are also sweet talkers (it is like you plant sugar cane beside the lips).

Repeat the sales promotion until you feel like throwing up. If the prospect is tough, change the script or pass it on to a senior.

24) HOSPITALIZED IN THE PSYCHIATRIC WARD

There was such intense emotional pressure on me at that time that I became excessively stressed.

Before anything bad happened, I went by myself to the emergency department at the hospital.

I met the doctor and spoke intermittently while crying. The doctor asked a few questions.

Blood sugar readings were taken, and the results were very high. HIGH.

My hand was pricked for the process of intravenous insertion. Two bottles. A few hours in the emergency department.

From late afternoon until midnight. The doctor had not made any decisions yet.

From a far, a doctor was observing me. Perhaps he was thinking about my condition, whether it was serious or not.

I spent a week in the psychiatric ward. Interacting with other mental patients. It enlightened me.

As bad as I am, there are others worse off. I received treatment for Bipolar disorder and diabetes simultaneously.

Doctors visited in shifts. The treatment provided was indeed the best.

I am entering the ward in the middle of the night, have been given hospital clothes, and have handed over my phone to a nurse.

Patients from various races. We were greeting each other as if we had known each other for a long time.

I was given a new medication to test its suitability and also diabetes treatment to lower my blood sugar levels.

I was given a menu as a diabetic patient. But surprising enough, I could finish all the food, especially the fruits.

I have been interviewed by a group of doctors, including resident doctors. My routine here is eating and sleeping.

Sometimes crying while walking around the ward for hours. When I am tired, I will sleep.
Wake up to eat and bathe. Most of the medication given causes me severe drowsiness.

TIMELINE: 2021-2023

RAY OF LIGHT

25) MARRIAGE

There is still someone who cares. If it is meant to be, it will be.

"I have diabetes. I'm afraid it might trouble you later". I confessed to my potential spouse when we first met.

"It's okay with me. My mother also has diabetes". She replied to me casually. When there is mutual interest, that is how it goes.

I was not satisfied yet. I still had doubts. I did not want my weaknesses and faults to become liabilities in this marriage.

"I have Bipolar disorder!" I stated firmly to my future wife. I also revealed my mental illness to her.

I would rather resign myself if she rejected me at that time.
It's better to be upfront from the beginning than to spark a war after marriage.

"I'm okay with that. My best friend has ADHD," she replied back casually without any surprise.

26) HOSPITALS

The journey of changing treatment locations due to relocation provided a different dimension to facing Bipolar symptoms.

It started at the Hospital Universiti Sains Malaysia (HUSM) in Kubang Kerian, Kelantan, Malaysia.

The treatment here was quite good. Here I was referred to MENTARI. A kind of occupational therapy. I was taught how to relax.

There were specific movements to calm the mind. I was taught how to apply for jobs.

There were also certain classes, like cooking. Making and selling cakes and snacks. I was also taught how to work.

When I returned to Kuala Lumpur to try working under the supervision of my brother-in-law (if not, I might have continued to rot in the village), I received psychiatric treatment at Hospital Kuala Lumpur (HKL).

I had to retell everything from the beginning about my illness. The medication given was still the same as HUSM.

Epilim Chrono, 500mg. Its effect? My mood become stabilized, but it felt empty and dull.

I neither get angry nor get sad. Before, anger and sadness would alternate.

When I was warded to Hospital Selayang, several appointments were made at this hospital before I requested to be transferred to Hospital Tuanku Jaafar (HTJ).

At HTJ, the PSY tried to give me different medications that did not suit me. So, I stuck with Epilim Chrono.

When I returned to my hometown, I resumed my treatment at HUSM. Then I applied for an OKU card (for physically or mentally disabled person) at the Department of Social Welfare.

I migrated to Kuala Lumpur when I got married and I received treatment at Hospital Universiti Kebangsaan Malaysia (HUKM) until nowadays.

MENTAL HEALTH

What is Mental Health?

To understand mental illness, the first thing we should do is we must understand what mental health is.

The World Health Organization (WHO) defines mental health as the ability to realize one's potential, cope with the normal stresses of life, work productively, and contribute to the community.

Adolescents are happier with their families, have better social interactions, can learn effectively, and can enjoy new experiences if they are mentally healthy.

The first few years of adolescence are where mental health should be nurtured and personality patterns established before transitioning into adulthood.

Mental illness poses a serious health threat in both developed and developing countries.

The National Health and Morbidity Survey (2011) shows that approximately 1 million (20%) children aged between 5 and 16 experience mental health problems such as developmental disabilities, emotional, and behavioral disorders.

What is Mental Disorder?

A mental disorder is a group of illnesses that can affect a person psychologically.

This can hinder one's ability to focus, interact, perform basic tasks, or enjoy life in general.

There are various types of mental disorders, including:

- **Anxiety Disorders** – Post-Traumatic Stress Disorder (PTSD), Obsessive-Compulsive Disorder (OCD)

- **Mood Disorders** – Clinical Depression and Bipolar Disorder

- **Psychotic Disorders** – Schizophrenia

- **Eating Disorders** – Bulimia and Anorexia Nervosa

- **Developmental Disorders** – Attention Deficit Hyperactivity Disorder (ADHD)

- **Behavioral Disorders** – Oppositional Defiant Disorder (ODD)

- **Intellectual Disabilities** – Autism Spectrum Disorder (ASD)

Signs of Mental Illness

Most adolescents with mental illness show sudden changes in their behavior or habits. These changes can occur suddenly or gradually. Some of the symptoms include:

- Withdrawal and loss of interest in others.

- Significant decline in abilities, especially at school or work, such as quitting sports, failing in school, or having difficulty performing routine tasks.

- Problems with concentration, memory, or logical thinking and speech that are difficult to explain.

- Loss of initiative or desire to participate in any activities.

- Feeling disconnected from oneself or the environment.

- Anxiety or suspicion towards others or strong feelings of worry.

- Strange behavior.

- Dramatic changes in sleep patterns and appetite or a decline in personal hygiene.

- Sudden mood changes.

- Weight loss and loss of appetite.

<u>*Self-Healing*</u>

Being tested with mental illness is also one of life's tests.

In the early stages of the illness, I completely did not understand and was confused about life, especially as a teenager who just began to explore the real world.

As I grew older, with life experiences, tests came and went calmly.

We are not unaffected, but we cannot control what will happen to us.

However, we can control ourselves. Our response to life's tests.
That is what sets us apart from others. Tests will always be present for everyone. The difference lies in the type, place, and time of the test. The fact is that no one is exempt from tests.

So, why be afraid of tests? Tests should not be asked for, but if they come, face them as they are.

It is an opportunity to gain rewards effortlessly. There are many ways to self-heal to ease the burden of life's tests.

Some people like to go to the beach and enjoy the breeze and the gentle lapping of waves while walking along the shore.

Some go into the forest, enjoying the vast greenery. Listening to the slow flow of the river is quite soothing to the soul.

For me, I often go to the beach nearby my house. I also ride a bicycle to the nearby river in my village. When I am in Kuala Lumpur, I always drive my car or ride my motorcycle to Bukit Ampang. The view is breathtaking, needless to say.

Sometimes I buy "nasi berlauk Air Dingin" and drive to Genting Highlands for breakfast at 'Batu Berayun' where is this place that not many people know when they going up Genting Highlands. The location is right before reaching the peak of Genting Highlands. The rock is huge, and I suspect it is made of cement. But if it is a natural rock, it is truly amazing.

Bathing in cool river water is very enjoyable.

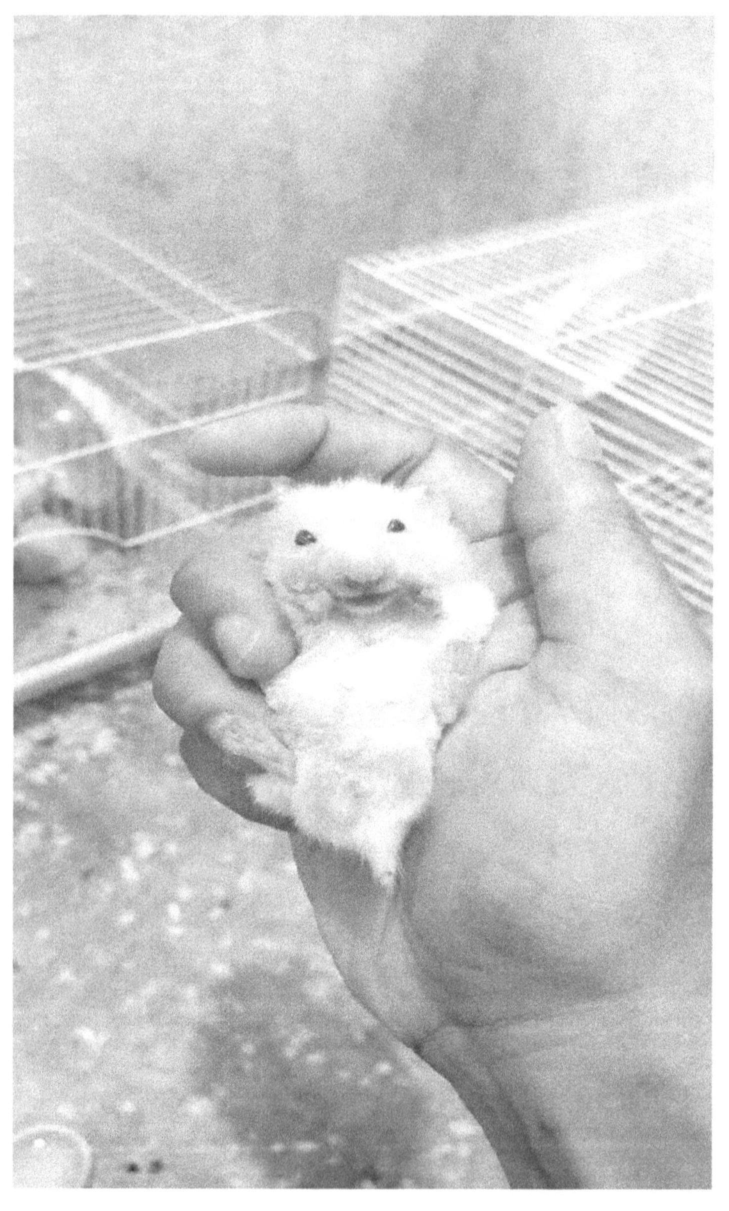

I raise hamsters. The feeling is different. Watching it run and chase around in its cage can lift up my mood and make me happy. Cute, small, and easy to care for, it becomes my choice for therapy.

For Muslims, the greatest self-healing is through prayer. It is not just about going through the motions but about praying with true focus and understanding, done with humility and a profound connection.

To achieve this focus, it requires time and some level of knowledge, starting from performing ablution.

As the water flows over the body during ablution, followed by preparation for prayer, it's a moment to detach briefly from the world and face our Creator.

From the first Takbir, the mind focuses on experiencing every subsequent step in the prayer.

With the second Salam, a sense of tranquility envelops the soul. Praying with both the body and spirit yields a feeling that cannot be expressed.

This is the greatest remedy for everything, especially for those battling mental illness.

For those struggling with mental illness, know that you are not alone.

Allah is with us, closer to us than our jugular vein. To feel this closeness, seek His guidance. Eventually, we will feel how close Allah is to us.

For parents struggling to raise their children, pay attention to their behavior.

They are a trust, not our possession. Trust is a responsibility. Do not let them face the critical teenage years alone.

The risk of rebellion is high, and emotions are easily disturbed. Do not let their mental health suffer due to our neglect.

For society as a whole, understand that those with mental illness are not crazy.

We just have some unseen problems. Help us with unwavering support.

We did not ask for this illness. Look around you, whether your neighbors, colleagues, relatives, or anyone else.

Are they okay? If someone tends to isolate themselves, seems sad, or is easily angered, talk to them.

Ask them what their problems are. Listening to them express themselves is also therapy for those with mental illness.

Do not let it worsen, because the worst thing that can happen is suicide.

Finally, I have successfully finished my writing about a little bit of my life story as a Bipolar Type 2 patient.

My struggles may not compare to those out there. Writing is therapy for me. What has happened is fate. I accept this fate with gratitude.

Thank you for taking your time to read my book. Your support means a lot to me.

If you don't mind, please share the link of my book to your friends, family, and others to spread its benefits while helping me reduce my financial burden.